# OLYMPIC
# TRIVIA

## By Marty Gitlin

SportsZone
An Imprint of Abdo Publishing
abdopublishing.com

**abdopublishing.com**

Published by Abdo Publishing, a division of ABDO, PO Box 398166, Minneapolis, Minnesota 55439. Copyright © 2016 by Abdo Consulting Group, Inc. International copyrights reserved in all countries. No part of this book may be reproduced in any form without written permission from the publisher. SportsZone™ is a trademark and logo of Abdo Publishing.

Printed in the United States of America, North Mankato, Minnesota
082015
012016

THIS BOOK CONTAINS
RECYCLED MATERIALS

Cover Photo: Julie Jacobson/AP Images
Interior Photos: Julie Jacobson/AP Images, 1, 4; Gero Breloer/AP Images, 7; Sergei Grits/AP Images, 9; Gerry Broome/AP Images, 11; Daniel Ochoa De Olza/AP Images, 12; Kyodo/AP Images, 14; Paul Vathis/AP Images, 17; Owen Humphreys/Press Association/AP Images, 19; AP Images, 21, 22, 29, 32, 36, 40, 43; Lennox McLendon/AP Images, 25; John Gaps III/AP Images, 27; Charles Dharapak/AP Images, 31; Dusan Vranic/AP Images, 35; Al Behrman/AP Images, 39

Editor: Patrick Donnelly
Series Designer: Jake Nordby

**Library of Congress Control Number: 2015945861**

**Cataloging-in-Publication Data**
Gitlin, Marty.
 Olympic trivia / Marty Gitlin.
   p. cm. -- (Sports trivia)
 ISBN 978-1-68078-005-5 (lib. bdg.)
 Includes bibliographical references and index.
 1. Olympics--Miscellanea--Juvenile literature.   2. Sports--Miscellanea--Juvenile literature.   I. Title.
 796.48--dc23

                                        2015945861

# CONTENTS

**T**he Olympic Games are more than just a sporting event. They are more than a showcase for great athletes. They are a symbol of unity and peace for all countries.

The Games have featured many of the finest athletic feats of all time. The modern Summer Games began in 1896. The Winter Olympics launched in 1924. How much do you know about the Olympics? Keep reading to find out!

*All statistics and answers are current through the 2014 Winter Olympics.

# CHAPTER 1

## ROOKIE

**Q** In which sport did Lindsey Vonn win a gold medal in 2010?

**A** Vonn won gold in the women's Alpine skiing downhill event. The downhill is the fastest event in Alpine skiing. Vonn is Team USA's most decorated female Alpine skier. She also has won many other Alpine skiing races outside the Olympics. Vonn might have been even more successful if not for a series of injuries she suffered.

**Q** When did football debut in the Olympics?

**A** Men's football became an Olympic sport in 1900. But not the football that is popular in the United States. North

Lindsey Vonn after her run in the women's downhill at the 2010 Winter Olympics

Americans call it soccer. Women's soccer debuted in the Olympics in 1996. American football has never been part of the Olympics.

**Q In which sport did the United States upset a powerful Soviet Union team in 1980?**

A US ice hockey players achieved that feat. The Soviets had won the previous four Olympic gold medals. They were considered the best in the world. But Team USA pulled off one of the greatest upsets of all time. The Americans beat the mighty Soviets 4–3. Two days later, they beat Finland to clinch the gold medal.

**Q Which indoor sport played with paddles has China dominated?**

A The Chinese have no peer in table tennis. Both individual play and doubles debuted in the 1988 Summer Games. In 2008 doubles was discontinued, but team competition was added. The Chinese men won four of five individual gold medals from 1996 to 2012. They also won team gold in 2008 and 2012. The Chinese women earned

every individual gold from 1988 to 2012. And they won

team gold medals in 2008 and 2012.

**A** The modern Olympic era dates back to the 1896 competition in Athens, Greece. The Olympic Games are based off an ancient Greek event. Baron Pierre de Coubertin of France wanted to revive the Olympics. He created the International Olympic Committee (IOC) in 1894. Two years later, 241 athletes from 14 nations gathered in Athens. They competed in 43 events.

**Q** Which US snowboarder nicknamed "The Flying Tomato" won gold in 2006 and 2010?

**A** Red-headed Shaun White became the first two-time gold medalist in the halfpipe. White began snowboarding at age six. He became the best in the world. Snowboarding had been popular with fans of extreme sports for years. Olympic snowboarding competition began in 1998.

**Q** What colors are the three medals awarded for every Olympic event?

**A** They are gold, silver, and bronze. But it was not always that way. Medals were not awarded in the ancient

Games in Greece. Instead, an olive branch was given to the winner of each event. At the first modern Games in 1896, the winners received a silver medal. Second-place finishers won a bronze medal. Gold, silver, and bronze medals were first presented in 1904 in St. Louis.

## Q How often do the Olympics take place?

A The Olympic Games are held every four years. However, the Summer Games and Winter Games are held two years apart. That means there is an Olympics every two years. Previously, the Summer and Winter Games were held in the same year. That changed in the early 1990s. Due to the change, Winter Games were held in 1992 and then again in 1994.

### WHICH US SWIMMER HOLDS THE ALL-TIME RECORD FOR MOST OLYMPIC GOLD MEDALS?

Michael Phelps set that record in 2012. He earned his first medal in the 2000 Games. Then he just kept winning. He won six gold medals in 2004. He won eight more in 2008. Phelps won his last four gold medals in 2012, bringing his count to 18. His 22 total Olympic medals is also a record.

## Q Who won four gold medals in track and field at the 1936 Olympics?

A Jesse Owens achieved one of the greatest feats in Olympic

The Canadian men's hockey team poses after winning the gold-medal game in 2014 in Sochi, Russia.

history in Munich, Germany. The US sprinter won four gold medals in track and field. He took first place in the 100- and 200-meter dashes. He won the long jump. And he anchored Team USA's winning 400-meter relay team.

**Which country won six of the first seven gold medals in ice hockey?**

**A** Canada won gold in every Olympics but one from 1920 to 1952. It lost in the finals to Great Britain in 1936. The Soviet Union then took control. It won seven of the next nine. Canada recovered to capture the gold in 2002, 2010, and 2014. The United States took gold in 1960 and 1980.

**Q** **Which sport features athletes shooting arrows at targets?**

**A** Archery became a modern Olympic sport in the 1972 Summer Games. US archers won five of the first eight men's gold medals. South Korea won four of the first seven men's team gold medals in archery. The United States won team gold in 1996.

# CHAPTER 2

# VETERAN

**Q** Who was the first gymnast to score a perfect 10 in the Olympics?

**A** Nadia Comaneci was just 14 years old when she made history in 1976. Her performance on the uneven bars was hailed as the greatest in Olympic history. The Romanian also won gold in the balance beam and floor exercise events at the 1980 Summer Games.

**Q** Which was the first US city to host the Olympic Games?

**A** St. Louis, Missouri, hosted both the Olympics and the World's Fair in 1904. Chicago had received the original bid to host the 1904 Games. But it was moved

Nadia Comaneci dismounts at the end of her perfect-10 performance in 1976.

to St. Louis to combine the two events. At that time, St. Louis was the fourth-largest city in the United States. Only New York, Chicago, and Philadelphia were larger.

**Q  Which is the largest US city to have never hosted the Summer Olympics?**

A New York City has never hosted the Summer Games. The only US cities that have are Los Angeles, St. Louis, and Atlanta. New York submitted a bid to host the 2012 Games. But the IOC instead chose London, England.

**Q  Eight of the top 15 women's gymnastics medalists come from which country?**

A Russia dominated the sport in the 1950s and 1960s. The greatest of all Russian gymnasts was Larisa Latynina. She earned a combined 18 medals in 1956, 1960, and 1964. Polina Astakhova won 10 medals in those same years. Six other Russian gymnasts are in the top 15 in Olympic history.

The women's marathon pack heads past Big Ben during the 2012 Summer Games in London.

**Q Which European city has hosted the Summer Olympics three times?**

A London hosted the fourth modern Olympics in 1908. It also hosted the Summer Games in 1948 and 2012. Paris was the first city to host the Summer Olympics twice. But it has not hosted the Games since 1924.

**Q** What is the official motto of the Olympic Games?

**A** The motto is "Faster. Higher. Stronger." Dominican priest Henri Didon introduced the phrase. He used it to open a school sports event in 1881. Coubertin was in the audience. When he founded the IOC, he remembered that phrase. But it was not used as the official Olympic motto until 1924.

**Q** What did US swimmer Mark Spitz achieve in the 1972 Olympics?

**A** He won an Olympic record seven gold medals. His record stood until 2008 when Phelps won eight. Spitz set world records in the 100-meter freestyle, 200-meter freestyle, 100-meter butterfly, and 200-meter butterfly in 1972. He also won two gold medals in the 1968 Olympics.

**Q** Which song is played during the medal ceremony after an event?

A The national anthem of the gold-medal winner is played.

The United States has won more gold medals than any

other country since the beginning of the modern Olympic

Bob Beamon shatters the long jump record in 1968.

Games. That means "The Star-Spangled Banner" has been the most played song in Olympic history.

**Q  Why were there no Olympic Games held in 1940 or 1944?**

**A** The world was at war in those years. Many countries were fighting in World War II (1939–1944). Among them were the United States, the Soviet Union, Great Britain, France, Japan, and Germany. Many of the finest athletes in the world joined the fighting. Some were killed in the war.

## WHO SHATTERED THE LONG JUMP WORLD RECORD AT THE 1968 SUMMER GAMES?

American Bob Beamon did more than just beat the world record. He destroyed it. Beamon soared 29 feet, 2 1/2 inches (8.90 m). The old record had been 27 feet, 4 3/4 inches (8.35 m). Beamon's leap remained the world record for 22 years. It is still the longest jump in Olympic history.

# CHAPTER 3

## CHAMPION

**Q** Which US athlete won nine gold medals in track and field between 1984 and 1996?

**A** Carl Lewis participated in four Summer Games, during which he earned gold nine times. He twice helped set world records in the 400-meter relay. Lewis also set an Olympic record in the 100- and 200-meter dashes. He even won gold in the long jump in 1996 at age 35.

**Q** What do the five rings on the Olympic design symbolize?

**A** The symbol represents the union of five continents. The rings are colored blue, yellow, black, green, and red. Coubertin designed the rings in 1913 to represent the

Carl Lewis soars to the gold medal in the
long jump in 1988.

flags of all nations. Every nation's flag has at least one of the five colors in it.

**Q** Which country won the most medals in the first modern Olympic Games?

**A** Host nation Greece earned the most overall medals in 1896 with 47. The United States won the most gold medals with 11.

**Q** What nickname did US men's basketball players embrace in the 1992 Summer Games?

**A** They were called "The Dream Team." That year National Basketball Association (NBA) players could take part in the Olympics for the first time. The US team included all-time greats such as Michael Jordan, Larry Bird, and Magic Johnson. The Dream Team outscored its eight Olympic opponents by nearly 44 points per game. The gold-medal game was no contest. The Dream Team beat Croatia 117–85 in the finals.

**Charles Barkley, *right*, entertains Chris Mullin, *center*, and John Stockton during the Dream Team's gold medal ceremony.**

**Q** **Which legendary American boxer won gold at the 1960 Summer Olympics?**

**A** Cassius Clay defeated Poland's Zbigniew Pietrzykowski for the gold in 1960. Clay then went on to become one of the greatest professional boxers of all time. He later changed his name to Muhammad Ali when he converted to Islam.

**Q** Who was the first black athlete to win an individual gold medal in the Winter Olympics?

**A** US speedskater Shani Davis won gold in the 1,000-meter event in 2006 and 2010. Davis was only four years old when he began ice skating. He emerged as one of the greatest black athletes in Winter Olympic history. In addition to his two gold medals, he won silver in the 1,500-meter race both years.

**Q** Which US swimmer won five Olympic gold medals in the 1920s before playing the role of Tarzan in the movies?

**A** That was Johnny Weissmuller, one of the greatest swimmers of all time. He won the 200- and 400-meter freestyle in 1924. He also won the 100-meter freestyle in 1928. Weissmuller went on to Hollywood and starred in 12 Tarzan movies.

**Q Which US discus thrower was the first athlete to win gold in four Olympic Games?**

A Al Oerter won every discus gold medal from 1956 to 1968. In a meet outside the Olympics in 1962, he became the first to heave the discus beyond 200 feet (61 m). At that time, he had already won two Olympic gold medals in the discus. He would win two more.

**Q Which Winter Olympic team was featured in the 1993 movie *Cool Runnings*?**

A The Jamaican bobsled team created a stir by qualifying for the 1988 Olympic Games in Calgary, Canada. Jamaica is a tropical island nation. It does not snow there. The Jamaicans did not come close to winning a medal. But fans and media were fascinated by their unique story.

**Q Which martial art has featured seven of the nine heaviest Olympic athletes?**

A Judo competitors can come in all sizes—even large ones. Ricardo Blas Jr. of Guam weighed 463 pounds

(210 kg) when he participated in the 2008 Summer Games. In 2004, 435-pound (197-kg) Aytami Ruano of Spain competed. Five other judokas are among the nine heaviest Olympians of all time.

Jim Thorpe was a star in many different sports.

32

**Q** Why did the United States boycott the 1980 Summer Olympics held in the Soviet Union?

**A** The Soviet Union invaded Afghanistan in 1979. The United States and many other nations opposed this move. So they boycotted the Games in protest. The Soviets returned the favor in 1984. Citing security concerns, they boycotted the Summer Olympics in Los Angeles.

## WHICH US ATHLETE IS CONSIDERED BY MANY THE GREATEST ATHLETE OF ALL TIME?

Jim Thorpe captured the gold medal in the decathlon and pentathlon in the 1912 Summer Games. King Gustav of Norway reportedly called him the greatest athlete in the world at the time. But Thorpe was just getting warmed up. He also played professional baseball and became a football star. In 1950 The Associated Press named Thorpe "The Greatest Athlete of the First Half of the Century."

# CHAPTER 4

## HALL OF FAMER

**Q** **Who was the tallest athlete ever to compete in the Olympics?**

**A** Yao Ming played basketball for the Chinese team in 2000, 2004, and 2008. He stood 7 feet, 6 inches (2.29 m) tall. He also played eight seasons in the NBA before injuries cut his career short. Yao was China's flag bearer at the 2008 Games in his home country.

**Q** **Who was the British ski jumper who memorably finished last at the 1988 Winter Olympics?**

**A** Eddie "The Eagle" Edwards was a popular Olympic athlete. He was also one of the least successful. The Eagle was the first ski jumper from Great Britain ever to

Yao Ming, *right*, grabs a rebound in front of Spain's Pau Gasol during the 2004 Olympics.

participate in the Games. He admitted he had no chance to win a medal. And he was right. Edwards finished last. But his charm, humility, and sense of humor won him many fans throughout the world.

**Q Which Greek god did the ancient Olympics honor?**

A They were held in honor of Zeus, the king of the Greek gods. The ancient Olympic Games were more of a religious festival than sporting event. A sacrifice of 100 oxen was made to Zeus during the event. Athletes prayed to the gods for victory.

**Q Which country has won the most medals in the modern Winter Olympics?**

A Norway holds that record with 329. That nation has also earned the most Winter Olympic gold medals with 118. The United States is second in both categories with 282 total

**WHO IS THE ONLY ATHLETE EVER TO WIN A GOLD MEDAL IN BOTH THE SUMMER AND WINTER OLYMPICS?**

Eddie Eagan won a gold medal in boxing at the 1920 Summer Games. But he hurt his hand in the 1924 Olympics. The injury ended his boxing career. He then trained with the American four-man bobsled team. He made history by winning gold in that sport in 1932.

medals and 96 gold. Austria is third in overall medals with 218. Russia is third in gold with 78.

**Q** **Which island nation won three of the five gold medals in baseball from 1992 to 2008?**

**A** Cuba earned gold in 1992, 1996, and 2004. Cuba's government did not let its players leave the country to play Major League Baseball. But some defected. Shortstop Alexei Ramirez and pitcher Jose Contreras both played on the Cuban Olympic team and in the major leagues.

**Q** **Which decathlete was the youngest track and field champion in Olympic history?**

**A** Bob Mathias was just 17 when he won the decathlon in 1948. In 1952, the American became the first to win the decathlon twice. Daley Thompson of Great Britain matched his two decathlon wins in 1980 and 1984. But Mathias remained the youngest winner of an Olympic track and field event.

**Q** **Why is a flock of doves released at the start of every Summer Olympics?**

**A** Doves are a symbol of peace. That makes them an ideal symbol for an event featuring the nations of the world.

Doves were first used as part of the opening ceremony after World War I (1914–1918).

Q **What nickname was given to the high-jump style popularized by 1968 US gold medalist Dick Fosbury?**

A The "Fosbury Flop" changed the high jump forever. Fosbury created the new jump in which he cleared the bar headfirst and backward. That allowed him to improve his leaps by a foot in high school. His jump of 7 feet, 4 1/4 inches (2.24 m) in the 1968 Games set Olympic and American records. The Fosbury Flop is now used by all high jumpers.

Q **What did Russian rower Vyacheslav Ivanov do with his silver medal in 1956?**

A He accidentally dropped it into a lake. Ivanov was half of a Russian duo that took silver at the Summer Games held in Australia. After being handed the medal, he let it slip through his fingers. Ivanov dove into the lake but could not find his medal. A 13-year-old boy named

Andrew Hemingway eventually did. He returned it to Ivanov, who gave him a box of Russian medals as a reward.

A Bob Hayes is the first person to win an Olympic gold medal and a Super Bowl ring. He won the 100-meter dash at the 1964 Games in Tokyo. A year later, he was a star wide receiver for the Dallas Cowboys. The Cowboys won the Super Bowl in 1972. Hayes was inducted into the Pro Football Hall of Fame in 2009.

# TRIVIA QUIZ

**1** Which French skier earned gold in all three Alpine events at the 1968 Games?

a. Franck Piccard

b. Henri Oreiller

c. Jean Vuarnet

d. Jean-Claude Killy

**2** Who in 1984 became the first US woman to win gold in the all-around gymnastics competition?

a. Carly Patterson

b. Shannon Miller

c. Mary Lou Retton

d. Gabrielle Douglas

**3** Which country was the first in South America to be chosen to host any Olympic Games?

a. Brazil

b. Argentina

c. Chile

d. Uruguay

**4** Which island nation off the Florida coast won all three medals in the 2008 women's 100-meter dash?

a. Ivory Coast

b. Jamaica

c. Cuba

d. Bahamas

**5** Which American diver hit his head on the diving board in one attempt at the 1988 Games and still won a gold medal?

a. Richard Rydze

b. Bruce Kimball

c. Greg Louganis

d. David Boudia

**6** Which Summer Olympic sport features categories for saber, foil, and epee?

a. Fencing

b. Equestrian

c. Sailing

d. Archery

**7** In which Winter Olympic sport do athletes use a broom to create a path for a stone sliding down the ice?

a. Luge

b. Halfpipe

c. Curling

d. Snowboarding

**8** Which island country—the largest one in the world—hosted the 1956 and 2000 Summer Games?

a. Greenland

b. Australia

c. New Zealand

d. Cuba

**9** Which Summer Olympic sport tests the skills of horseback riders?

a. Equestrian

b. Fencing

c. Cricket

d. Polo

*Answers on page 47

# GLOSSARY

**anchor**
The last leg of a relay race.

**boycott**
Refusal to participate in an event or purchase a product, often for political reasons.

**decathlon**
A competition at the Summer Olympics that combines 10 track-and-field events.

**freestyle**
A swimming event in which competitors can use whichever stroke they prefer.

**professional**
In sports, an athlete who is paid to perform.

**sprinters**
Track-and-field athletes who run short distances as fast as they can.

**symbolize**
To stand for or represent a concept or idea.

**upset**
An event in which the team or individual expected to lose instead wins the competition.

**venue**
The city or place in which an event is held.

# For More Information

## Books

Hunter, Nick. *The Winter Olympics*. Portsmouth, NH: Heinemann Publishing, 2013.

Lawrence, Blythe. *Great Moments in Olympic Gymnastics*. Minneapolis, MN: Abdo Publishing, 2015.

McDougall, Chrös. *Jesse Owens: Trailblazing Sprinter*. Minneapolis, MN: Abdo Publishing, 2011.

## Websites

To learn more about Sports Trivia, visit **booklinks.abdopublishing.com**. These links are routinely monitored and updated to provide the most current information available.

## Answers

| | | | |
|---|---|---|---|
| 1. | d | 6. | a |
| 2. | c | 7. | c |
| 3. | a | 8. | b |
| 4. | b | 9. | a |
| 5. | c | | |

# INDEX

## About the Author

Marty Gitlin is a freelance author and sportswriter. He has had approximately 100 books published, mostly in the realm of sports. He won more than 45 awards as a newspaper sportswriter, including first place for general excellence from the Associated Press. Gitlin lives with his wife and three children in Cleveland, Ohio.